TIM TEBOW
Football Superstar

BY MATT DOEDEN

CAPSTONE PRESS
a capstone imprint

Sports Illustrated Kids Superstar Athletes is published by Capstone Press,
1710 Roe Crest Drive, North Mankato, Minnesota 56003.
www.capstonepub.com

Library of Congress Cataloging-in-Publication Data
Tim Tebow : football superstar / by Matt Doeden.
p. cm.—(Sports illustrated kids. superstar athletes)
Includes index.
ISBN 978-1-62065-623-5 (library binding)
ISBN 978-1-62065-624-2 (paperback)
1. Tebow, Tim, 1987—Juvenile literature. 2. Football players—United States—Biography—
Juvenile literature. 3. Quarterbacks (Football)—United States—Biography—Juvenile literature.
I. Title. II. Series.
GV939.T423D64 2013
796.332092—dc23   2012014233

Editorial Credits

Anthony Wacholtz, editor; Kazuko Collins, designer; Eric Gohl, media researcher;
    Eric Manske, production specialist

Photo Credits

Getty Images/Jeff Zelevansky, cover (right): New York Jets/Al Pereira, cover (left), 19
Newscom/ZUMA Press, 9
Sports Illustrated/Al Tielemans, 1, 2–3, 16, 22 (middle); Bill Frakes, 22 (bottom); Bob Rosato, 12, 24;
    Damian Strohmeyer, 22 (top); Heinz Kluetmeier, 10; Peter Read Miller, 6, 15, 21;
    Robert Beck, 5, 23

Design Elements

Shutterstock/chudo-yudo, designerpix, Fassver Anna, Fazakas Mihaly

Direct Quotations

Page 7: Rick Mease. "NFL playoffs 2012: Tim Tebow, Denver Broncos Eliminate Pittsburgh Steelers in OT."
Washington Post. 8 Jan 2012. 17 May 2012. www.washingtonpost.com/sports/redskins/nfl-playoffs-2012-tim-
tebow-denver-broncos-upset-pittsburgh-steelers-in-ot/2012/01/08/gIQATvqFkP_story.html

Page 18: Rich Cimini. "Tim Tebow Meets New York Media." ESPN.com. 26 March 2012. 17 May 2012. http://
espn.go.com/new-york/nfl/story/_/id/7738997/new-york-jets-tim-tebow-says-mark-sanchez-work-together

Printed in the United States of America in North Mankato, Minnesota.

042013   007264R

TABLE OF CONTENTS

CHAPTER 1

OVERTIME THRILLER

It was the first play of overtime in the National Football League (NFL) playoffs in 2012. Denver Broncos quarterback Tim Tebow stood behind his line. It was the biggest game of his pro career. Few experts had thought the Broncos could even stay close to their opponents, the Pittsburgh Steelers. But now a touchdown would win the game.

Tebow took the snap. He stepped back and looked down the field. Then he saw his man. He threw the ball toward wide receiver Demaryius Thomas. Tebow's pass was right on target. Thomas caught it and turned on the speed. The Pittsburgh defenders couldn't catch him. Touchdown! The Broncos had won. Tebow charged down the field to celebrate the win with his team.

**"We knew that it was win or go home. And this team wanted to fight."
— Tim Tebow**

CHAPTER 2

BECOMING A CHAMPION

Timothy Richard Tebow was born August 14, 1987, in Makati City, Philippines. His parents were there as **missionaries**. The family later returned home to Florida.

Tebow and his four siblings were homeschooled. He was allowed to play football for Nease High School. He became one of the best quarterbacks in the nation. He led Nease to a state championship.

missionary—a person sent by a church or religious group to teach others about a certain religion

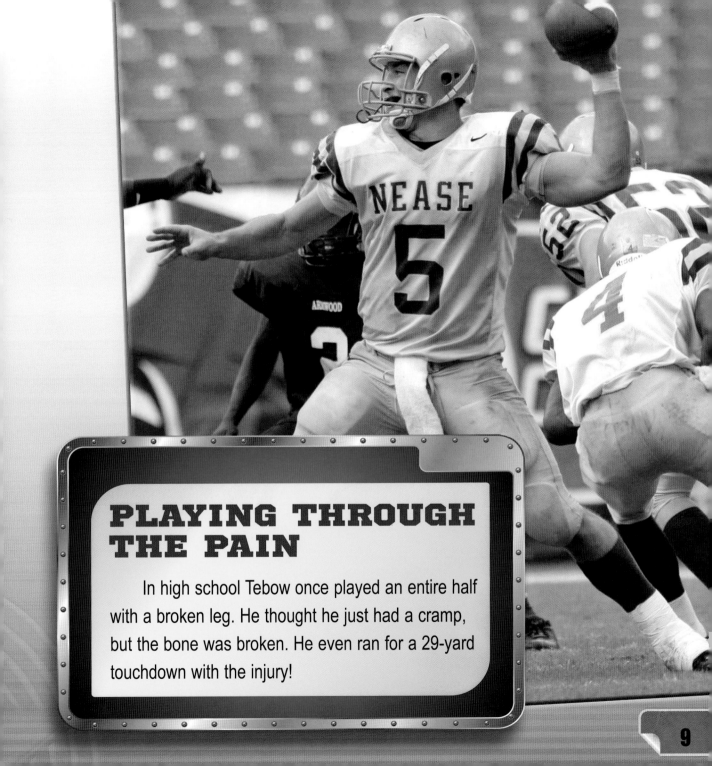

PLAYING THROUGH THE PAIN

In high school Tebow once played an entire half with a broken leg. He thought he just had a cramp, but the bone was broken. He even ran for a 29-yard touchdown with the injury!

College coaches around the nation wanted Tebow. He accepted a **scholarship** to play football at the University of Florida. He was a backup in his first year. But he still played a lot. Florida won the national championship. Tebow threw a touchdown pass and ran for another touchdown in the title game.

scholarship—money provided for a student's education

Tebow went on to become one of the greatest players in Florida history. He won two national titles with the Gators. In 2007 he became the first sophomore to win the **Heisman Trophy**. He also became the only Gator to win the team's Most Valuable Player Award three times.

Heisman Trophy—an award given to the best college football player each year

CHAPTER 3

WELCOME TO THE NFL

Some **scouts** questioned Tebow's future in the NFL. They thought he lacked the arm strength to be a starting quarterback. Some said he should switch to another position. But the Denver Broncos disagreed. They selected him in the first round of the 2010 NFL **Draft**. Tebow was the backup quarterback. He started three games that year.

scout—a person who evaluates athletes' talent and potential
draft—a process by which teams select new players

Tebow was the backup quarterback again at the beginning of the 2011 season. But he got the starting job after six weeks. Opposing teams never knew whether he would run the ball or pass it. The Broncos started winning. Tebow led several exciting comebacks. He started getting a lot of attention from fans and the media. The excitement was called Tebowmania.

The Broncos made the playoffs after the 2011 season. Tebow helped them to a thrilling victory over the Pittsburgh Steelers. But the Broncos lost to the New England Patriots the next week. In the offseason the Broncos signed star quarterback Peyton Manning. They traded Tebow to the New York Jets soon after.

"I'm excited to be a Jet and help this team in any way that I can."
— Tim Tebow

CHAPTER 4

TEBOWMANIA

Tebow was unsure what his role would be with the Jets. But he remained confident. One thing is for sure. Tebow is one of a kind among today's NFL quarterbacks. Only time will tell whether he has what it takes to become a truly great quarterback.

TEBOWING

Tebow often kneels on the field to pray. Fans started calling this pose "Tebowing." The pose quickly became a craze among sports fans.

TIMELINE

1987—Tebow is born August 14 in Makati City, Philippines.

2005—Tebow plays for Nease High School in Ponte Vedra and is named Florida's High School Player of the Year for the second time in a row.

2006—Tebow attends the University of Florida and helps the Florida Gators win the National Championship.

2007—Tebow wins the Heisman Trophy, becoming the first sophomore to win the award.

2008—Tebow leads the Gators to another National Championship.

2009—Tebow graduates from the University of Florida with a degree in family, youth, and community sciences.

2010—The Denver Broncos select Tebow in the first round of the NFL Draft.

2011—Tebow takes over as the Broncos starting quarterback and leads them to the playoffs.

2012—The Broncos trade Tebow to the New York Jets.

GLOSSARY

draft (DRAFT)—a process by which teams select new players

Heisman Trophy (HIZE-muhn TROH-fee)—an award given to the best college football player each year

missionary (MISH-uh-ner-ee)—a person sent by a church or religious group to teach others about a certain religion

scholarship (SKOL-ur-ship)—money provided for a student's education

scout (SKOUT)—a person who evaluates athletes' talent and potential

READ MORE

Doeden, Matt. *Greatest Sports Stars*. Sports Illustrated Kids. Mankato, Minn.: Capstone Press, 2011.

Frisch, Aaron. *New York Jets*. Super Bowl Champions. Mankato, Minn.: Creative Education, 2011.

Stewart, Mark. *The Florida Gators*. Team Spirit. Chicago: Norwood House Press, 2011.

INTERNET SITES

FactHound offers a safe, fun way to find Internet sites related to this book. All of the sites on FactHound have been researched by our staff.

Here's all you do:

Visit *www.facthound.com*

Type in this code: 9781620656235

Check out projects, games and lots more at
www.capstonekids.com

INDEX